The History and Untold Story of Evergrande China and its Liquidation

Navin Vett

Table Of Contents

Evergrande China

The second-largest real estate developer in China based on sales is the China Evergrande Group. Its headquarters are in the Houhai Financial Center in Nanshan District, Shenzhen, Guangdong Province, China, and it was formed in the Cayman Islands, a British Overseas Territory. In 1996, when (Xu Jiayin) started it. Most of the people that buy apartments from it are middle-class and upper-class.

It rose to the top of the global real estate value rankings in 2018, but by 2021 it had gone bankrupt and sparked the real estate market meltdown.
Evergrande Group filed for bankruptcy in New York on August 17, 2023. A Hong Kong court ordered their liquidation on January 29, 2024.

Past Events
During a time of widespread urbanization in China, Hui Ka Yan launched Evergrande, formerly known as the Hengda Group, in the southern metropolis of Guangzhou in 1996.

The business raised $723 million US in October 2009 through an IPO on the Stock Exchange of Hong Kong.

The Chinese real estate sector crisis of 2020–2023 was sparked by Evergrande's 2021 debt obligations, which were anticipated to be in the hundreds of billions of dollars. In September 2021, a number of stock market indices saw a decline due in part to this.

It was stated at the end of 2021 that the Chinese government was trying to fix the situation by restructuring Evergrande. In January 2022, the business requested from its bondholders a ban on the early repayment option on one of its yuan-denominated notes. The business declared in 2022 that it will relocate its head office to Guangzhou in order to cut costs.

Reports from a popular news source in April 2022 stated that the corporation still owed US$300 billion in liabilities despite the fact that work had resumed on some projects.

Evergrande disclosed to the public on July 17, 2023, that it had incurred a financial loss of 105.8 billion yuan (US$14.6 billion) in 2022 and 475 billion yuan (US$66.2 billion) in 2021.
According to the group, as of December 31, 2022, its total liabilities were 2.42 trillion yuan, or about US$330 billion. In July 2023, court sessions concerning the group's debt restructuring were scheduled to take place in Hong Kong and the Caribbean.

Evergrande filed for protection from creditors under Chapter 15 of the US bankruptcy code with the US bankruptcy court in Manhattan in August 2023. Evergrande's stock fell 78% to 35 HK cents when trading returned to Hong Kong in August 2023, following a 17-month suspension. This was in contrast to the pre-suspension price of HK$1.65 in March 2022.

Bloomberg revealed in September that police have taken control of Hui Ka Yan, the billionaire head of Evergrande. According to Caixin, Pan Darong, the former chief financial officer of Evergrande, and Xia Haijun, the former CEO, have been taken into custody by Chinese authorities.

Activities and commercial objectives

The Evergrande Group is the owner of real estate projects and development land of 564 million square meters (6,079 million square feet) spread throughout 22 cities in Mainland China, including Guangzhou, Tianjin, Nanning, and Guiyang.
One of the company's notable projects is Ocean Flower Island in Hainan.

In Mainland China, Evergrande Real Estate holds the second position in terms of real estate development. Along with the other two of the top three real estate firms, Vanke and Country Garden, it is referred to as "Wan Heng Bi". The company has created projects in more than 169 Chinese Mainland cities.

2014 saw the completion of Chengdu's Evergrande Plaza, which was created by Aedas.

Travel And Leisure

Hengda Children of the World and Hengda Water World are two of Evergrande's well-known theme park brands. Hainan is home to the sizable tourism complex "Chinese island of Hainan to spend."One of its main projects is the Ocean Flower Island in Hainan, which is now under construction.

Athletics

It purchased Guangzhou Evergrande F.C., a football team, in 2010 and made significant investments to sign elite players. With Marcello Lippi in charge, the team won the 2013 AFC Champions League. Additionally, Alibaba owns 55% of the football team.

In Xie Village, Panyu District, Guangzhou, Evergrande began building the Guangzhou Evergrande Football Stadium in April 2020.

A football tutoring school is called Evergrande Football School.
The Guangdong Evergrande Volleyball Club's women's team was sponsored by the corporation, who ended their eight-year agreement in October 2021.

Automobile

Using its Evergrande Health subsidiary, Evergrande paid $2 billion to acquire a 44% share in Faraday Future, an electric vehicle manufacturer, in 2018.

The business and State Grid Corporation of China teamed together in July 2019 to build charging stations for electric vehicles.

In November 2019, Evergrande made an announcement stating that it would invest ¥45 billion over the next three years to develop new energy vehicles, construct three production bases in Nansha, Guangzhou, and Shanghai, and introduce electric vehicles under the "Evergrande New Energy Vehicle" brand in 2020, thereby establishing the Hengchi electric vehicle brand.

Evergrande Group paid $381million for the remaining 49% of NEVS in June 2020. The group had previously paid $932 million for 52% of the shares in 2019. .

Well-being

Evergrande purchased New Media Group Holdings in March 2015 and changed its name to Evergrande Health. In Nanning, the Evergrande Health Valley" is run by Evergrande Health Group.

The Health Valley is a retirement community and park focused on health and wellness. Additionally, it collaborates with Massachusetts' Brigham and Women's Hospital to oversee Boao Evergrande International Hospital in Hainan.

Evergrande Health is a listed corporation as well as a division. But in August 2020, the part of the firm that was listed was rebranded as China Evergrande New Energy Vehicle Group Limited.

As of 2021, the health section remains a part of China Evergrande New Energy Vehicle Group Limited, which is a subset of the Evergrande Group.

Amusement

In 2015, HengTen Networks was established in collaboration with Tencent. HengTen Networks declared in October 2020 that it will pay HK$7.1 billion to purchase Ruyi Pictures. Tencent purchased a 7% share in HengTen from the company in August 2021 for US$417 million.Evergrande's association with Tencent came to an end when it sold off the remaining portion of its share in HengTen later in 2021.

Money

Sino-Singapore Great Eastern Life Insurance Company was renamed Evergrande Life after Evergrande paid $616 million to purchase a 50% ownership in the company in November 2015. Additionally, it owns stock in Shengjing Bank. Customers have also purchased wealth management products from Evergrande.

Agriculture and food

The Evergrande Group invested ¥5.55 billion in its "Hengda Bingquan" (later renamed "Evergrande Spring") mineral water brand in 2014 and hired Jackie Chan to promote it. Customers in Korea were particularly critical of Evergrande's water brand since the water source was stated as "Jang bai shan" (Changbai mountains) on the label rather than the more common Korean moniker, "Mount Baekdusan." There is tension between China and South Korea over the usage of the mountain's Chinese name, despite it bordering both countries.

Evergrande sold its agriculture units, which included its grain and oil company, dairy business, and mineral water brand, for ¥2.8 billion in September 2016, following a ¥4 billion loss. Subsequently, Evergrande declared later in the year that it would be spending ¥300 million to construct over 112 pig farms in the southwest region of Guizhou province.

Money Issues

The liquidity problem of Evergrande
Due to the publication of a highly critical report on the company, the Hong Kong Market Misconduct Tribunal suspended American short seller and founder of Citron Research Andrew Left for five years in 2016.

The tribunal found Left guilty of disclosing false or misleading information that could have caused transactions under the Securities and Futures Ordinance (SFO) in a research report on Evergrande Real Estate Group Limited (Evergrande) published in June 2012. Regarding speech freedom in Hong Kong's financial sector, the trading ban has sparked worries.

The business was encouraging staff members to buy financial products from the corporation even as it was dealing with a cash crunch.

Restrictions on the real estate market were implemented by the administration of CCP General Secretary Xi Jinping in 2020, with the rationale being that "property is to be lived in, not to be speculated on."

The Evergrande liquidity crisis occurred in the summer of 2021 as a result of payments on its debt, which is projected to be in the hundreds of billions of dollars. In September 2021, a number of stock market indices saw a decline due in part to this.

Evergrande declared in October 2021, that a planned $2.5 billion asset sale to settle a $82 million interest payment it missed in September 2021 had fallen through. November 10, 2021.

After missing the interest payment grace period, Evergrande went into default on three more debts. Major financial media sites have been citing anonymous sources regarding the bond payments since September, therefore even if major news outlets claimed they fulfilled the payments after the deadline, these claims cannot be independently verified.

Even if the amount of debt was enormous in November 2021, Evergrande has not yet reached "insolvency" based only on financial data. As per the financial report noted earlier, Evergrande's land reserve was valued at RMB 456.7 billion. When combined with 147 previous reform projects, the land reserve's overall worth approached RMB 2 trillion. In addition, there are other finished commercial holdings and properties, including the RMB 10 billion headquarters building in Hong Kong.

Trading in Evergrande shares was halted in September 2023, following the publication of a report claiming that Hui, the company's chairman, was the subject of a police investigation over possible criminal activity.

January 29 2024

China Evergrande Group was ordered to be liquidated by a Hong Kong court on Monday January 29 . As policy makers struggle to handle the worsening crisis, this decision is expected to have an impact on China's collapsing financial markets.

When Evergrande, the developer with the largest overall debt in the world (more than $300 billion), missed payments on its loan in 2021, it completely collapsed the already precarious real estate market.

This exacerbated the sector's financial crisis and led to numerous other firm defaults, causing a severe blow to the economy that continues to hinder growth to this day. The developer, whose assets total $241 billion, faces a liquidation order that is expected to upset the already unstable Chinese real estate and finance markets.

Beijing is now battling an underperforming economy, the worst real estate market in nine years, and a stock market that is languishing close to five-year lows. As a result, any new negative impact on the markets could jeopardize efforts by authorities to spur development.

The numerous authorities participating in the liquidation process may make it difficult and give rise to political concerns.

However, given that mainland China is a different legal jurisdiction from Hong Kong, it may take months or years for the offshore liquidator appointed by the creditors to take control of subsidiaries there, it is anticipated to have little effect on the company's operations, including home construction projects, in the near future.

With the ad hoc bondholder group, Evergrande had been working on a $24 billion debt reform plan for nearly two years. When it announced in late September that its rich creator, Hui Ka Yan, was being investigated for possible crimes, it ruined its first plan.

Top Shine, an investor in the Evergrande company Fengshibao, initially filed the liquidation petition in June 2022, claiming the developer had broken a deal to buy back shares it had purchased in the subsidiary.

Judge Linda Chan of the Hong Kong High Court had earlier stated that the December hearing would be the final one before a decision was made about the liquidation of Evergrande in the absence of a "concrete" restructuring plan. The proceedings had been postponed numerous times.

Since the present financial problem began to emerge in mid-2021, a Hong Kong court had ordered at least three Chinese developers to liquidate before Monday.

Even as authorities work to stop a selloff in the Chinese stock market, the liquidation order is expected to have an effect on China's financial system.

A Hong Kong court ordered China Evergrande Group to liquidate on Monday, January 29, 2024, after the company was unable to come to a restructuring agreement with its creditors.
Given Evergrande's insolvency and the "lack of progress on the part of the company putting forward a viable restructuring proposal," **Judge Linda Chan** declared that the court had the right to order the company to wind up its operations.

Even as authorities work to stop a selloff in the Chinese stock market, the liquidation order is expected to have an effect on China's financial system. The property industry has been experiencing a decline in confidence due to developers' inability to fulfill their obligations after the industry clamped down on excessive borrowing. Evergrande's liquidation is expected to contribute to this decline.

After declaring that it was working to "refine" a fresh debt restructuring plan involving more than $310 billion in obligations, Evergrande was given a brief reprieve in December.

An **ad hoc** group of creditors' attorney, **Fergus Saurin**, once stated he was not surprised by the result.

"The business has not communicated with us." There have been previous instances of last-minute engagements that ended in failure.
Saurin stated that Evergrande "only has itself to blame for being wound up" and that his team had been operating in good faith the entire time.

During a second court session on Monday afternoon, the judge is anticipated to give additional justification for the liquidation decision.
The most indebted real estate developer in the world, Evergrande, is only one of many real estate companies that faced difficulties as Chinese regulators clamped down on excessive borrowing in the real estate industry.

Only a little over a year after Beijing tightened down on loans to real estate developers in an attempt to quell a property bubble, the company first fell behind on its financial obligations in 2021.

China's economic development was fueled by real estate, but when builders transformed cities into forests of residential and office towers, they took on a lot of debt. Due to this, total debt held by corporations, governments, and households has increased to an exceptionally high level for a middle-income nation—more than 300% of yearly economic production.

A number of other firms, notably Country Garden, the biggest real estate developer in China, have also had difficulties, with their problems spreading throughout international banking networks.

The aftermath of the real estate crisis has also had an impact on China's shadow banking sector, which consists of companies like Zhongzhi Enterprise Group that offer banking-like financial services but are not subject to banking laws. Zhongzhi declared itself insolvent after making large loans to developers.

Evergrande Group's History

1996

During a time of widespread urbanization in China, Hui Ka Yan launched Evergrande, formerly known as the Hengda Group, in the southern metropolis of Guangzhou in 1996.

The second-largest real estate developer in China based on sales is the China Evergrande Group. Its headquarters are in the Houhai Financial Center in Nanshan District, Guangdong Province, China, and it was formed in the Cayman Islands, a British Overseas Territory. In 1996, Hui Ka Yan (Xu Jiayin) started it. Most of the people that buy apartments from it are middle-class and upper-class.

It rose to the top of the global real estate value rankings in 2018, but by 2021 it had gone bankrupt and sparked the real estate market meltdown.

October of 2009

The business raised $723 million US in October 2009 through an IPO on the Stock Exchange of Hong Kong.

2010

It purchased Guangzhou Evergrande F.C., a football team, in 2010 and made significant investments to sign elite players. With Marcello Lippi in charge, the team won the 2013 AFC Champions League. Additionally, Alibaba owns 50% of the football team.

June of 2012

Due to the publication of a highly critical report on the company, the Hong Kong Market Misconduct Tribunal suspended American short seller and founder of Citron Research Andrew Left for five years in 2016.

The tribunal found Left guilty of disclosing false or misleading information that could have caused transactions under the Securities and Futures Ordinance (SFO) in a research report on Evergrande Real Estate Group Limited (Evergrande) published in June 2012.

The New York Times claims that the trading prohibition "has raised concerns over freedom of speech in Hong Kong's financial markets."
2014 Aedas designed and finished Chengdu's Evergrande Plaza in 2014.

2014

The Evergrande Group invested ¥5.55 billion in its "Hengda Bingquan" (later renamed "Evergrande Spring") mineral water brand in 2014 and hired Jackie Chan to promote it.

Customers in Korea were particularly critical of Evergrande's water brand since the water source was stated as "Jang bai shan" (Changbai mountains) on the label rather than the more common Korean moniker, "Mount Baekdusan." There is tension between China and South Korea over the usage of the mountain's Chinese name, despite it bordering both countries.

2015
In 2015, HengTen Networks was established in collaboration with Tencent. HengTen Networks declared in October 2020 that it will pay HK$7.3 billion to purchase Ruyi Pictures. Tencent purchased a 7% share in HengTen from the company in August 2021 for US$419 million.

Evergrande's association with Tencent came to an end when it sold off the remaining portion of its share in HengTen later in 2021.

March of 2015
Evergrande purchased New Media Group Holdings in March 2015 and changed its name to Evergrande Health. In Nanning, the Evergrande Health Valley" is run by Evergrande Health Group. The Health Valley is a retirement community and park focused on health and wellness.
Additionally, it collaborates with Massachusetts' Brigham and Women's Hospital to oversee Boao Evergrande International Hospital in Hainan.

November of 2015
Sino-Singapore Great Eastern Life Insurance Company was renamed Evergrande Life after Evergrande paid

$617 million to purchase a 50% ownership in the company in November 2015.

Additionally, it owns stock in Shengjing Bank. Customers have also purchased wealth management products from Evergrande.

September of 2016

Evergrande sold its agriculture units, which included its grain and oil company, dairy business, and mineral water brand, for ¥2.8 billion in September 2016, following a ¥4 billion loss. Subsequently, Evergrande declared later in the year that it would be spending ¥300 million to construct over 112 pig farms in the southwest region of Guizhou province.

October of 2017

S&P Global formally declared Evergrande in default in December 2021, following the company's failure to make a bond payment earlier that month. Evergrande shares were taken out of trade in January 2022, with no explanation given by the business.

A day later, trading was reopened, and the stock price increased by 10%. Evergrande's share price fell to a new all-time low of HK$1.16 on March 15, 2022, from a peak of more than HK$31 in October 2017.

2018

Using its Evergrande Health subsidiary, Evergrande paid $2 billion to acquire a 45% share in Faraday Future, an electric vehicle manufacturer, in 2018.

2019

Evergrande Group paid $380 million for the remaining 49% of NEVS in June 2020. The group had previously paid $931 million for 51% of the shares in 2019.

2020

The administration of CCP General Secretary Xi Jinping began to restrict the real estate market in 2020, basing its policies on the tenet that "property is to be lived in, not to be speculated on." The property market declines as a result of new regulations, with sales falling by 30% in 2021.

2020 April

In Xie Village, Panyu District, Guangzhou, Evergrande began building the Guangzhou Evergrande Football Stadium in April 2020.

August of 2020

Evergrande Health is a listed corporation as well as a division. But in August 2020, the part of the firm that was listed was rebranded as China Evergrande New Energy Vehicle Group Limited.

2021

The Chinese real estate sector crisis of 2020–2023 was sparked by Evergrande's 2021 debt obligations, which were anticipated to be in the hundreds of billions of dollars. In September 2021, a number of stock market indices saw a decline due in part to this. It was stated at the end of 2021 that the Chinese government was trying to fix the situation by restructuring Evergrande. On January 7, 2022, the business requested from its bondholders a ban on the early repayment option on one of its yuan-denominated notes.

2021

In 2021 and 2022, the corporation suffered losses of 477 billion and 106 billion yuan, respectively.

September 2021

The Evergrande liquidity crisis occurred in the summer of 2021 as a result of payments on its debt, which is projected to be in the hundreds of billions of dollars. In September 2021, a number of stock market indices saw a decline due in part to this.

Evergrande declared on October 21, 2021, that a planned $2.6 billion asset sale to settle a $83 million interest payment it missed in September 2021 had fallen through. Evergrande's default on three additional bonds occurred on November 10, 2021, as a result of missing the interest payment grace period.

Major financial media sites have been citing anonymous sources regarding the bond payments since September, therefore even if major news outlets claimed they fulfilled the payments after the deadline, these claims cannot be independently verified.

October of 2021

The Guangdong Evergrande Volleyball Club's women's team was sponsored by the corporation, who ended their eight-year agreement in October 2021.

November 2021

Even if the amount of debt was enormous in November 2021, Evergrande has not yet reached "insolvency" based only on financial data. As per the financial report noted earlier, Evergrande's land reserve was valued at RMB 456.9 billion.

When combined with 146 previous reform projects, the land reserve's overall worth approached RMB 2 trillion. In addition, there are other finished commercial holdings and properties, including the RMB 10 billion headquarters building in Hong Kong.

2022

The business declared in 2022 that it will relocate its head office to Guangzhou in order to cut costs.

March of 2022

Evergrande announced on March 30, 2022, that it would sell its Crystal City Project in Hangzhou to Zhejiang Zhejiang Real Estate Group and Zhejiang Construction Engineering Group for 3.66 billion yuan.

The proceeds of the sale will be used to pay off Zhejiang Construction Engineering's 920.7 million yuan construction debt. There should be a gain of almost 216 million yuan from the transaction.

April of 2022

Reports from Reuters in April 2022 stated that the corporation still owed US$300 billion in liabilities despite the fact that work had resumed on some projects.

December 2022
Evergrande disclosed to the public in July 2023, that it had incurred a financial loss of 105.9 billion yuan (US$14.7 billion) in 2022 and 476 billion yuan (US$66.3 billion) in 2021.
According to the group, as of December 31, 2022, its total liabilities were 2.43 trillion yuan, or about US$340 billion. In July 2023, court sessions concerning the group's debt restructuring were scheduled to take place in Hong Kong and the Caribbean.

August 2023
Evergrande Group filed for bankruptcy in New York in August 2023. A Hong Kong court ordered their liquidation in January 2024.

August 2023
Evergrande filed for Chapter 15 bankruptcy in New York in August 2023.

14 August 2023
NWTN Group made its first strategic investment of $500 million in Evergrande Group on August 14, 2023.

September of 2023

Trading in Evergrande shares was halted in September 2023, following the publication of a report claiming that Hui, the company's chairman, was the subject of a police investigation over possible criminal activity.

Evergrande was constructing a new stadium for their football franchise, Guangzhou FC, prior to its financial difficulties.
The most indebted firm in the world is experiencing a worsening issue as a result of the authorities placing its chairman under surveillance.

It comes after earlier rumors that several executives from the Chinese real estate behemoth Evergrande, both current and past, had also been taken into custody.
It represents yet another low point for the company, which was deemed in default in 2021 after failing to meet a critical repayment date, which led to the current real estate market crisis in China.

Financial Woes

In Guangzhou, southern China, businessman Hui Ka Yan established Evergrande, originally the Hengda Group, in 1996.

On its website, Evergrande Real Estate claims to presently hold over 1,300 projects spread over more than 280 Chinese cities.

There is much more to the larger Evergrande Group than merely real estate development.

Its enterprises include wealth management, the production of electric vehicles, and the production of food and beverages. It even has a majority ownership in Guangzhou FC, one of the biggest football teams in the nation.

Mr. Hui was once the richest person in Asia; Forbes valued his fortune at $42.6 billion (£34.9 billion). However, since then, his wealth has drastically decreased, mostly due to the worsening of Evergrande's issues.

What is the problem with Evergrande?
By borrowing more than $300 billion, Evergrande rapidly grew to become one of the largest enterprises in China.

Beijing implemented new regulations in 2020 to limit the amount that large real estate developers owed.

Evergrande was forced by the new regulations to give steep discounts on its properties in order to guarantee revenue flow and maintain operations.
It is currently having difficulty making the interest payments on its loans.

Evergrande's shares have lost 99% of their value over the last three years due to this uncertainty.
The company filed for bankruptcy in New York in an effort to safeguard its US assets while negotiating a multibillion-dollar agreement with creditors.

Why does the collapse of Evergrande matter?
Evergrande's issues are severe for a number of reasons.
First off, a lot of individuals purchased real estate from Evergrande prior to the start of construction. They have made deposits, and should it fail, they might lose their funds.

Additionally, there are the businesses that deal with Evergrande. Businesses that supply materials, such as design and construction firms, run the danger of suffering significant losses that might push them into bankruptcy.

The third is the possible effect on the Chinese financial system: banks and other lenders would be compelled to reduce their lending if Evergrande fails.

This might result in a credit crunch, which is characterized by businesses finding it difficult to obtain loans at reasonable interest rates.
The second largest economy in the world would suffer greatly from a credit crisis since businesses that are unable to borrow find it difficult to expand and sometimes even cease operations.

This can also frighten international investors, who might think China is a less desirable destination for their capital.

'Too big to fail', is Evergrande?
Some observers have speculated that Beijing would intervene to save the corporation due to the extremely dangerous potential consequences of such a highly indebted company failing.
Evergrande is on the verge of a forced liquidation. "To be honest, Evergrande has already collapsed,"

Given that the property industry accounts for over 25% of China's economic development, this might have a significant impact on the country's economy.
The nation may be headed in the same direction that Japan did when it entered decades of economic stagnation in the 1980s.

Some, meanwhile, believe it is doubtful that Evergrande will be permitted to fall apart entirely.

"That could spiral, affecting other indebted companies and further hurt the overall property sector which is very important to the growth of the economy,"
"At the same time, many people whose household wealth is mainly in their apartments will also be badly hurt,"

While the authorities may manage to keep the old Evergrande afloat, "it will be as a radically diminished company." The old Evergrande has long since vanished.

Prior to the Liquidation

What You Should Know About China's Troubled Real Estate Giant, Evergrande

Despite the company's enormous debts, Beijing will have to tread carefully if it is to safeguard its economy and send a lesson about careless borrowing.

Every now and then a business gets so large and disorganized that governments worry about the potential effects on the overall economy should it fail. That company is Evergrande, a large-scale real estate developer in China.

Evergrande is the developer with the highest debt load in the world and has been on life support for some months. It appears that it is currently dealing with Asia's largest business restructuring.

The Chinese developer has not fulfilled its contractual duties. According to Evergrande, representatives from a number of state-sponsored organizations have formed a risk committee that will assist the business in restructuring.

Evergrande is a massive real estate conglomerate that owns millions of flats in several hundred Chinese cities. In addition, it has hundreds of unfinished residential structures, more than $300 billion in financial liabilities, and irate suppliers who have closed down construction sites. The situation deteriorated to the point that the corporation paid its past-due payments with incomplete properties and requested loans from its staff.

What occurs next may have an impact on hundreds of thousands of workers who work for the company, property buyers, and more than 3.8 million jobs in China.

As for Beijing's plans to clean up the business sector by allowing "debt bombs" like Evergrande to collapse, observers are now keeping an eye on how the company manages its next chapter.

Was Evergrande in default?
Evergrande kept the financial markets on edge for months by completing bond payments at the last minute, narrowly avoiding multiple instances of default. But Evergrande announced on December 3 that it was unlikely to continue meeting its financial obligations due to increasing pressure and a lack of funds to keep operations running.

Following another deadline for two bond payments that passed without any indication of payment or communication from Evergrande, Fitch Ratings categorized the Chinese developer as being in its "restricted default" category the following week.

The category indicates that although Evergrande had officially fallen behind, it had not yet filed for bankruptcy, gone into liquidation, or engaged in any other procedure that would have forced it to cease operations.

This would allow creditors to file a lawsuit to try to recover their money in the US and many other countries. However, investors are waiting to see what strategy could emerge because Chinese government authorities have closely monitored prior company meltdowns to ensure they don't escalate out of hand.

Evergrande announced that it would "actively engage" with its foreign creditors to devise a restructuring plan, which is typically a protracted and laborious process of dismantling a corporation and selling its components to satisfy all parties.
Assets located abroad may attract investors, but the process could be complicated.

"Evergrande is a complicated company with entities in both domestic and foreign businesses," "To reorganize the group, a clear-cut, unified legal method cannot be used. It will therefore need to span jurisdictions, which will add to its complexity.

How did Evergrande get to be a major issue?
Ten years ago, when Evergrande was at the top of its game, the company produced bottled water, owned China's top soccer team, and even tried its hand at pig farming for a short while. It grew to such an extent and became so expansive that it has an electric car division, albeit mass production has been postponed.

The largest banks in China now view Evergrande as a shaky danger.

Established in 1996, the company saw the tremendous real estate boom in China, which led to the urbanization of vast regions and the accumulation of almost 75% of household wealth in housing.
As a result, Evergrande became the dominant force in an economy that increasingly relied on the real estate sector to drive rapid economic expansion.

Xu Jiayin, the company's millionaire founder, is a member of the Chinese People's Political Consultative Conference, an exclusive network of influential advisers in politics.
Due to Mr. Xu's ties, creditors were probably more willing to continue giving money to Evergrande as the company grew and entered new markets. But eventually Evergrande found itself in debt beyond its means.

It has been the target of litigation in recent years from purchasers who have paid for apartments but are still waiting for them to be completed. Bills that are yet unpaid amount to hundreds of billions of dollars, according to suppliers and creditors. On certain Evergrande projects, building has been halted.

Why is the business suddenly having so many problems?

Should there not have been two issues, Evergrande might have been able to continue. First, authorities in China are taking harsh measures against developers who borrow money carelessly. Evergrande's massive commercial empire has to be sold off in part as a result, and things aren't going very well.

Despite discussions with potential buyers, it was unable to sell its electric car company. According to some analysts, consumers were holding out for a fire sale.
Second, there is less demand for new flats as China's real estate industry slows down. Noting poor demand and decreasing sales, the National Institution for Finance and Development, a well-known think tank in Beijing, claimed that the real estate market boom had "shown signs of a turning point."

As a result, China's economic development is generally slowing down, which might further reduce demand for Evergrande's real estate in a vicious cycle.

A significant portion of the funds that Evergrande has raised have come from pre-sold yet unfinished units. According to a Barclays estimate, Evergrande has about 810 incomplete projects throughout China and up to 1.7 million people who are still waiting to move into their new houses.

Will it be saved by Chinese regulators intervening?

For years, a lot of investors funded businesses like Evergrande on the assumption that Beijing would always bail them out if things got too unstable. And the investors were correct for many years.

Recently, though, the government has demonstrated a stronger readiness to allow businesses to fail in an effort to control China's unmanageable debt load.

Up until now, the government has been adamant about staying out of the way when it comes to developers. At least 11 developers have already fallen behind on their bond payments so far this year.

To accentuate this point, the situation is exclusive to Evergrande, according to China's central bank, which attributed the company's issues to "own poor management and reckless expansion." The governor of the central bank, Yi Gang, has said that a rescue for Evergrande was not likely.

What impact would Evergrande's demise have on the Chinese economy?

The central bank's efforts to curb real estate debt and lessen the banking industry's exposure to financially unstable developers could lessen the impact of an Evergrande catastrophe on China's financial system.

It's possible that reality is more nuanced.

Investor and homebuyer anxiety may seep into the real estate market, driving down prices and eroding consumer confidence and wealth. Additionally, it can cause tremors in the world's financial markets and make it more difficult for other Chinese enterprises to get foreign investment to fund their operations.

A collapse may cause a credit bottleneck that would affect the whole economy as banks become less risk-tolerant. The collapse of Evergrande was "not good news to the financial system or the overall economy."

However, not everyone has the same outlook. It might pave the way for a more robust economy down the road. Beijing's tolerance for defaults, even in the near term, will be demonstrated if Evergrande fails and the notion that it is "too big to fail" fades.

Do international investors need to worry?
Now, foreign investors are concerned that the money they owe could be locked in China and be hard to get out. They would be well down the list of creditors to receive any assets from the Chinese corporation in any bankruptcy proceeding.

Some, though, are more upbeat. The reasoning goes that since China Inc. has to be able to raise capital from outside investors, Beijing would ensure that bondholders may partially recoup their losses.

According to one estimate, foreign investors owed U.S. bond payments of $1.3 billion this month and $17 billion by April of next year.

Based in Hong Kong, Alexandra Stevenson covers business news on China's corporate behemoths, shifting conditions for international corporations, and China's expanding financial and economic sway over Asia. Additional information on Alexandra Stevenson

After Evergrande Liquidation

The developer will name a formal liquidator after a provisional liquidator to take charge and get ready to liquidate the developer's assets to pay off its obligations.

If the liquidators concluded Evergrande had sufficient assets or a white knight investor showed up, they might offer a new debt restructuring plan to offshore creditors holding $US 23 billion in debt in the company.
They might also look into the company's operations and report any alleged wrongdoing by directors to the prosecutors in Hong Kong.

A liquidation order might be challenged by Evergrande, but in the meantime, the liquidation process would continue.

But how much debt could be collected by creditors?
During a July court hearing in Hong Kong, Evergrande referenced a Deloitte research project that projected a 3.4% recovery rate in the event that the developers were liquidated.
After Ever Grande announced in September that the authorities were looking into its chairman, Hui Ka Yan, and flagship unit for "illegal crimes" that were not specifically stated, creditors now anticipate a recovery rate of less than 3%.

Experts stated that while the developer with $US240 billion in assets being wound up would cause tremors in the already unstable capital markets, it would not provide a template for how other struggling developers' liquidations would go.

Several authorities and political concerns would be involved in the process due to the enormity of Evergrande's projects and debt.
The corporation, the industry, and the government will place a high premium on finishing ongoing home construction projects.

www.ingramcontent.com/pod-product-compliance
Lightning Source LLC
Chambersburg PA
CBHW071017290526
45795CB00005B/1844